Smoker Cookbook

Delicious Smoker And Smoked Meat Recipes For Beginners

Copyright ©

All rights reserved. No part of this book may be reproduced, stored in a retrieval system, or transmitted in any form or by any means, electronic, mechanical, photocopying, recording, scanning, or otherwise, without the prior written permission of the publisher.

Disclaimer

All the material contained in this book is provided for educational and informational purposes only. No responsibility can be taken for any results or outcomes resulting from the use of this material.

While every attempt has been made to provide information that is both accurate and effective, the author does not assume any responsibility for the accuracy or use/misuse of this information.

You should always consult a doctor regarding any medical conditions, the information in this book is not intended to diagnose or treat any medical condition or illness.

Table of Contents

Introduction   1

Chapter 1: Smoked Pork Recipes   2

Chapter 2: Smoked Beef Recipes   27

Chapter 3: Smoked Chicken And Turkey Recipes   42

Introduction

Smoking meat is a fun and easy cooking experience that everyone should try. There are a variety of different kinds of smokers, and different methods for smoking meats. Smoking meats is one of my favorite cooking methods because it gives your meats much more flavor than your regular barbeque can. Below are a few tips for getting started.

Beginner Tips For Smoking Meat:

- Carefully choose your type of wood for smoking based on your taste and meat selection. You can use wood from almost any kind of fruit tree for smoking meat. Two of the most common woods used for smoking meats are hickory and apple wood. Hickory is a very strong and intense flavor, I mainly use hickory for pork, ribs, and beef. Apple wood is a much milder and sweeter flavor. I recommend experimenting with different kinds of woods to find your preference.

- It is best using wood that is six months old from when it was cut, this will provide better flavors.

- Use a instant read thermometer to check if meat is done. Insert the thermometer in the center of the meat for the best accuracy.

- Use heat resistant cooking gloves, your smoker will be very hot.

- Smoke your meat outdoors away from trees or buildings.

- Soak your wood chips in water to prevent flare ups.

- To prevent burning, apply the sauce on the meats in the last 15-30 minutes of cooking.

In this cookbook, I will share my favorite smoked meat recipes with you, there are a wide range of smoked meat recipes you can try.

Chapter 1: Smoked Pork Recipes

Spicy Smoked Pulled Pork

Ingredients

1 tablespoon mild paprika

2 teaspoons light brown sugar

1 1/2 teaspoons hot paprika

1/2 teaspoon celery salt

1/2 teaspoon garlic salt

1/2 teaspoon dry mustard

1/2 teaspoon ground black pepper

1/2 teaspoon onion powder

1/4 teaspoon salt

8 pounds pork butt roast

2 cups cider vinegar

1 1/3 cups water

5/8 cup ketchup

1/4 cup firmly packed brown sugar

5 teaspoons salt

4 teaspoons crushed red pepper flakes

1 teaspoon ground black pepper

1 teaspoon ground white pepper

2 pounds hickory wood chips, soaked

Directions

In a small bowl, mix mild paprika, light brown sugar, hot paprika, celery salt, garlic salt, dry mustard, ground black pepper, onion powder, and salt. Rub spice mixture into the roast on all sides. Wrap in plastic wrap, and refrigerate 8 hours, or overnight.

Prepare a grill for indirect heat.

Sprinkle a handful of soaked wood over coals, or place in the smoker box of a gas grill. Place pork butt roast on the grate over a drip pan. Cover grill, and cook pork until pork is tender and shreds easily, about 6 hours. Check hourly, adding fresh coals and hickory chips as necessary to maintain heat and smoke.

Remove pork from heat and place on a cutting board. Allow the meat to cool approximately 15 minutes, then shred into bite-sized pieces using two forks. This requires patience.

In a medium bowl, whisk together cider vinegar, water, ketchup, brown sugar, salt, red pepper flakes, black pepper, and white pepper.

Continue whisking until brown sugar and salt have dissolved. Place shredded pork and vinegar sauce in a large roasting pan, and stir to coat pork.

Serve immediately, or cover and keep warm on the grill for up to one hour until serving.

Simple Smoked Pork Butt

Ingredients

7 pounds fresh pork butt roast

2 tablespoons ground New Mexico chile powder

4 tablespoons packed brown sugar

Directions

If desired, soak the pork butt in a brine solution for at least 4 hours or overnight.

Preheat an outdoor smoker for 200 to 225 degrees F (95 to 110 degrees C).

In a small bowl, combine the brown sugar, chili powder and any additional seasonings to your taste. Apply this liberally to the meat and rub it in with your fingers. Place a roasting rack in a drip pan and lay the meat on the rack.

Smoke at 200 to 225 degrees F (95 to 110 degrees C) for 6 to 18 hours, or until internal pork temperature reaches 145 degrees F (63 degrees C).

Sweet Paprika Smoked Pork Ribs

Ingredients

1/4 cup salt

1/4 cup white sugar

2 tablespoons packed brown sugar

2 tablespoons ground black pepper

2 tablespoons ground white pepper

2 tablespoons onion powder

1 tablespoon garlic powder

1 tablespoon chili powder

1 tablespoon ground paprika

1 tablespoon ground cumin

10 pounds baby back pork ribs

1 cup apple juice

1/4 cup packed brown sugar

1/4 cup barbeque sauce

Directions

Stir salt, white sugar, 2 tablespoons brown sugar, black pepper, white pepper, onion powder, garlic powder, chili powder, paprika, and cumin together in a small bowl to make the dry rub. Rub the spice mixture into the baby back ribs on all sides. Wrap the ribs well with plastic wrap, and refrigerate for at least 30 minutes prior to cooking.

Unwrap baby back ribs and place onto the wire racks of the smoker in a single layer.

Place the racks into a smoker, fill the smoker pan with apple, grape, pear, or cherry chips, and bring the smoker to 270 degrees F (130 degrees C). Smoke for 1 hour.

Stir together the apple juice, 1/4 cup brown sugar, and the barbeque sauce. Brush the ribs with the sauce every 30 to 45 minutes after the first hour.

Cook the ribs in the smoker until the meat is no longer pink and begins to "shrink" back from the bones, 3 to 4 hours. Brush the sauce onto the ribs one last time 30 minutes before the ribs are ready to be taken out of the smoker.

Once the ribs are done, wrap them tightly with aluminum foil, and allow to rest 10 to 15 minutes. This will allow the juices to reabsorb into the meat and make the ribs moist.

Smoked Hickory Pork Shoulder

Ingredients

1 (8 pound) pork shoulder roast

1 quart apple cider, or as needed

5 tablespoons white sugar

5 tablespoons light brown sugar

2 tablespoons kosher salt

2 tablespoons paprika

1 tablespoon onion powder

1 tablespoon freshly ground black pepper

1 tablespoon garlic powder

1 onion, chopped

3 cups hickory chips, or more as needed, soaked in water

Directions

Place pork shoulder in a large pot and add enough apple cider to cover. Combine white sugar, brown sugar, salt, paprika, onion powder, black pepper, and garlic powder in a bowl. Mix about 1/4 cup sugar rub into cider; reserve remaining rub.

Cover pot and refrigerate for 12 hours.

Prepare smoker to about 210 degrees F (99 degrees C). Add enough wood chips to smoker.

Pour cider brine into the water pan of the smoker; add onion and about 1/4 cup more sugar rub. Spread remaining rub over pork shoulder. Transfer pork to the center of smoker.

Smoke pork until very tender, about 8 hours. Monitor hickory chips and liquid, adding more wood and water, respectively, as needed. Transfer pork to a large platter and cool for 30 minutes before shredding with forks.

Smoked Kielbasa Sausage

Ingredients

14 feet of natural pork casings

4 pounds of ground pork

½ cup water

2 garlic cloves, minced

4 teaspoons sea salt

1 teaspoon coarse black pepper

1 teaspoon marjoram

Directions

Mix the pork with water, garlic, and seasonings

Stuff the casings according to manufacturer's instructions on your sausage stuffer. Twist the casing into desired lengths or weight

Poke with a pin all over the sausage to prevent sausages from bursting.

Set the sausage in the refrigerator for one day to let the flavors combine.

To smoke the kielbasa, place in your smoker setup with your wood of choice.

Smoke for 2-3 hours. Make sure the sausages internal temperature is 155 F before removing.

Smoked Apple wood Bacon

Ingredients

4 pounds raw pork belly

1/2 cup packed brown sugar

1/4 cup sugar-based curing mixture

1 gallon cold water, or as needed

1 (10 pound) bag charcoal briquettes

Apple wood chips

Directions

In a 2 gallon container, mix together the brown sugar, curing mixture, and water. Submerge the pork belly in the mixture so that it is covered completely. If the meat floats, you can weigh it down with a dinner plate or similar object. Refrigerate covered for six days.

Light charcoal in an outdoor smoker. Soak wood chips in a bowl of water. When the temperature of the smoker is between 140 and 150 degrees coals are ready.

Smoke the pork belly for 6 hours, adding some wood chips on the coals about once an hour.

Store in the refrigerator.

Spicy Smoked Spare Ribs

Ingredients
6 pounds pork spareribs

2 cups wood chips, or as needed

Dry rub:
1/2 cup packed brown sugar

2 tablespoons chili powder

1 tablespoon paprika

1 tablespoon freshly ground black pepper

2 tablespoons garlic powder

2 teaspoons onion powder

2 teaspoons kosher salt

2 teaspoons ground cumin

1 teaspoon ground cinnamon

1 teaspoon jalapeno seasoning salt (optional)

1 teaspoon cayenne pepper

mop sauce:
1 cup apple cider

3/4 cup apple cider vinegar

1 tablespoon onion powder

1 tablespoon garlic powder

2 tablespoons lemon juice

1 jalapeno pepper, finely chopped (optional)

3 tablespoons hot pepper sauce

kosher salt and ground black pepper to taste

Directions

In a medium bowl, mix together the brown sugar, chili powder, paprika, black pepper, 2 tablespoons garlic powder, 2 teaspoons onion powder, kosher salt, cumin, cinnamon, jalapeno seasoning, and cayenne pepper. Rub generously onto the pork spareribs. Cover, and refrigerate for at least 4 hours, or overnight.

Prepare an outdoor grill for indirect heat, or preheat a smoker to 250 degrees F (120 degrees C) with oak wood chips.

While the grill heats, prepare the mop sauce. In a medium bowl, stir together the apple cider, apple cider vinegar, 1 tablespoon onion powder, 1 tablespoon garlic powder, lemon juice, jalapeno, hot pepper sauce, salt and pepper.

When the coals are gray and ashed over, place 2 handfuls of soaked woodchips directly on them. Place the ribs on the grill grate bone-side down. Cover, and cook for 3 1/2 to 4 hours. Add more coals as needed.

Baste with the mop sauce, and add handfuls of soaked woodchips onto the coals every hour. Keep the temperature of the grill or smoker from going below 225 degrees F (110 degrees C).

Ribs are done when the rub has created a crispy blackened skin, and the meat has pulled away from the bone. Discard any leftover mop sauce.

Smoked Maple Bacon

Ingredients

1 1/2 gallons water

2 tablespoons sodium nitrate

1 cup sugar-based curing mixture

2 cups coarse salt

1 cup packed brown sugar

1/2 cup maple syrup

1 (14 pound) whole pork belly

maple, apple, or cherry wood chips for smoking

Directions

Pour water, sodium nitrate, curing salt, coarse salt, brown sugar, and maple syrup into a large kettle. Bring to a boil over high heat and cook for 10 to 15 minutes until everything is well dissolved. Pour brine into a 5 gallon plastic bucket and cool to room temperature, 6 to 8 hours.

Leaving the skin on the pork belly, cut against the grain into 4 to 6 slabs so they fit inside the bucket, and inside your smoker. Place into the bucket of brine, and weigh down with a glass or ceramic dish to keep the pork submerged. Cover and refrigerate for 5 to 7 days, rearranging the pork in the brine daily.

On smoking day, remove pork from the brine and rinse well under cold running water, rubbing to remove all external brine. Pat pieces dry and place onto smoker racks. Allow pork pieces to stand, preferably underneath a fan, until the surface of the meat becomes somewhat dried and notably glossy, 1 to 3 hours depending on air circulation.

Smoke pork belly slabs using wood of your choice at a temperature of 90 to 110 degrees F (32 to 43 degrees C) for 8 to 12 hours. Remove rind before slicing.

Smoked Chipotle Pork Tenderloin

Ingredients

1 pork tenderloin

1/4 cup BBQ sauce

Chipotle Rub

2 tbsp chipotle powder

2 tbsp smoked paprika

1 tbsp garlic powder

1 tbsp cumin

1 tbsp coriander

2 tbsp salt

2 tbsp dark brown sugar

Directions

Start smoker, using wood of choice, setting the temperature of the smoker for 225F.

Trim pork tenderloin of any fat or silver skin. Generously rub the chipotle mix all over the meat.

Place meat in the smoker and smoke till the internal temperature is 145F, about 2 1/2 - 3 hours.

Brush the meat with BBQ sauce 30 minutes before removing from smoker.

BBQ Garlic Pork Ribs

Ingredients

5 pounds baby back pork ribs

1/2 gallon apple juice

1 head garlic, separated into cloves

1 tablespoon granulated garlic

2 cups barbeque sauce

Directions

Prepare charcoal in a smoker, and bring the temperature to 225 degrees F (110 degrees C).

Cut the ribs into smaller portions of 3 or 4 ribs, and place them in a large pot. Pour in enough apple juice to cover. Place a lid on the pot and bring to a boil. Remove from the heat, and let stand for 15 minutes.

Lightly oil the grate in your smoker. Place ribs on the grate, and throw a few cloves of garlic onto the hot coals. Close the smoker. Maintain the temperature at 225 degrees F (110 degrees C) by adding more charcoal as needed. Smoke the ribs for 7 hours, adding more garlic cloves to the coals occasionally.

Make a sauce by mixing together the barbeque sauce with 2 cups of the apple juice from the pot.

Season with granulated garlic. Baste ribs with this sauce while continuing to cook for another 30 minutes.

Smoked Garlic Pork Butt

Ingredients

1 (5- to 6-pound) butt pork roast

2 cups prepared mustard

1 1/2 cups ketchup

3/4 cup cider vinegar

2 tablespoons sugar

2 tablespoons Worcestershire sauce

1 tablespoon hot sauce

2 tablespoons butter

5 garlic cloves, chopped

2 tablespoons salt

1 tablespoon pepper

Hickory wood chips

Directions

Soak wood in water 1 hour.

Cook mustard and next 6 ingredients in a large saucepan over low heat, stirring often, 20 minutes; remove from heat, and set aside.

Cut several deep slits in roast using a paring knife. Stir together garlic, salt, and pepper; rub on all sides of roast.

Prepare charcoal fire in smoker; let burn 15 to 20 minutes.

Drain wood; place on coals. Place water pan in smoker; add water to fill line. Place pork roast in center of lower food rack. Pour 1 cup mustard mixture over roast.

Cook, covered with smoker lid, 6 to 7 hours or until a meat thermometer inserted into thickest portion registers 165°, adding additional wood and charcoal every hour as needed.

Remove roast from smoker; cool slightly. Chop and serve with remaining mustard sauce.

Smoked Pork Tenderloin With Herbs

Ingredients

2 1 pound pork tenderloins, trimmed

4 thin slices prosciutto

1/4 cup fresh breadcrumbs

2 tablespoons fresh parsley, minced

2 teaspoons fresh rosemary, minced

1 clove garlic, minced

2 tablespoons extra virgin olive oil

salt and pepper to taste

Directions

Set the temperature to 225 F, add a handful of cherry wood chips to the smoker box. Preheat your electric smoker for 40 minutes.

Place the tenderloins on a cutting board. Drape the prosciutto slices over one of the tenderloins with the slices hanging over the tenderloin on both sides.

Combine the breadcrumbs, parsley, rosemary and garlic. Spread evenly on top of the prosciutto. Fold over the ends of the slices, laying the second tenderloin on top.

Tie the tenderloins together using kitchen twice at about 1-inch intervals. Liberally salt and pepper the meat. Place the tenderloin on a rimmed foil-lined baking sheet.

Put the tenderloin in the smoker, attach the digital thermometer and set it for 145 degrees Fahrenheit.

Put the probe end of the thermometer in the thickest part of one of the tenderloin. Smoke until the internal temperature is reached. Let the tenderloin rest 10 minutes before removing the string and slicing.

Smoked Sweet BBQ Spare Ribs

Ingredients

2 slabs pork spare ribs

Dry rub

1/2 teaspoon cinnamon

1/2 teaspoon ground cloves

1/4 teaspoon pepper

BBQ sauce

2 15 ounce cans tomato paste

1/2 cup molasses

10 garlic cloves

2 tablespoons ground cumin

2 tablespoons dry mustard

fresh ground pepper

1/2 teaspoon cinnamon

1/4 teaspoon hot pepper flakes

Directions

Add cherry wood chips to the smoker and preheat your digital electric smoker.

While the smoker preheats, combine all dry ingredients for your dry rub. Combine all ingredients for barbecue sauce. Simmer, covered on low for about an hour and stirring occasionally. Save for later use.

Remove the membrane from the back of the ribs. Rub down both sides with the dry rub.

Place the ribs on smoker racks, setting the smoker to 225 F. Smoke until the internal temperature of ribs reaches about 170 degrees Fahrenheit.

Baste with BBQ sauce.

Chapter 2: Smoked Beef Recipes

Smoked Hickory Bourbon Rib Roast

Ingredients

15 pounds charcoal briquets

1 cup bourbon whiskey

1 (4 pound) standing rib roast, bone in

1/2 cup steak seasoning

2 pounds hickory wood chips

Directions

Start at least 10 pounds of the charcoal in a torpedo style smoker. Make sure it is a hot fire. Fill the secondary pan with cold water, and wait for the coals to turn white. Soak hickory chips in bourbon with enough water to cover. Rub the roast liberally with steak seasoning, making sure to coat all surfaces.

When the coals are ready, place the roast on the top grate. Throw a few handfuls of soaked hickory chips onto the fire, and close the lid. Check the fire every 45 minutes or so, adding more charcoal as needed to keep the fire hot.

Every time you check the fire, add more wood chips. Cook for 8 to 10 hours, or to your desired doneness. Use a meat thermometer to check the roast.

Paprika Smoked Beef Brisket

Ingredients

10 pounds beef brisket, or more to taste

1/4 cup paprika

1/4 cup white sugar

1/4 cup ground cumin

1/4 cup cayenne pepper

1/4 cup brown sugar

1/4 cup chili powder

1/4 cup garlic powder

1/4 cup onion powder

1/4 cup kosher salt

1/4 cup freshly cracked black pepper

wood chips

Directions

Soak wood chips in a bowl of water, 8 hours to overnight.

Mix paprika, white sugar, cumin, cayenne pepper, brown sugar, chili powder, garlic powder, onion powder, salt, and black pepper together in a bowl. Rub the spice mixture over the entire brisket; refrigerate for 24 hours.

Preheat smoker to between 220 degrees F (104 degrees C) and 230 degrees F (110 degrees C). Drain wood chips and place in the smoker.

Smoke brisket in the preheated smoker until it has an internal temperature of 165 degrees F (74 degrees C), about 12 1/2 hours. Wrap brisket tightly in butcher paper or heavy-duty aluminum foil and return to smoker.

Continue smoking brisket until an internal temperature of 185 degrees F (85 degrees C) is reached, about 1 hour more.

Smoked Corn Beef

Ingredients

1 (5 pound) beef brisket, fat trimmed to a thin layer

2 cups apple juice, or as needed

Brine:

3 quarts cold water

3 (12 fluid ounce) bottles lager beer

2 onions, cut into wide slices

1 1/2 cups kosher salt

1/2 cup dark brown sugar

5 tablespoons curing salt

1/4 cup pickling spice

2 tablespoons chopped garlic

Braising Liquid:

1 (12 fluid ounce) bottle lager beer

1 onion, cut into large slices

2 tablespoons dark brown sugar

2 tablespoons pickling spice

2 tablespoons chopped garlic

1 teaspoon ground black pepper (optional)

Directions

Place water, 3 bottles beer, 2 onions, kosher salt, 1/2 cup brown sugar, curing salt, 1/4 cup pickling spice, and 2 tablespoons garlic in a very large pot. Stir well until salts are dissolved. Add beef; stir gently. Use a large bowl or heavy plate to keep the beef submerged. Cover with plastic wrap and refrigerate, stirring once a day, for 4 days.

Soak wood chips in apple juice for 2 hours.

Remove beef from pot, discarding brine, and rinse well until cold water. Let beef come to room temperature.

Preheat an outdoor grill to 150 to 175 degrees F (65 to 80 degrees C). Place soaked wood chips in a shallow aluminum pan on the heat source.

Place meat directly on the grate and allow to smoke for 2 hours.

Combine 1 beer, 1 onion, 2 tablespoons brown sugar, 2 tablespoons pickling spice, 2 tablespoons chopped garlic, and black pepper in a large saucepan; bring to a boil. Remove from heat and pour into a large roasting pan. Place beef in braising liquid in the roasting pan and cover tightly with aluminum foil.

Increase grill temperature to 250 degrees F (120 degrees C). Place the roasting pan on the grill and close the lid.

Roast the beef until tender, 3 to 4 hours. An instant-read thermometer inserted into the center should read at least 145 degrees F (60 degrees C).

Remove beef from the roasting pan, discarding braising liquid. Let beef cool until easily handled.

Slice beef into very thin slices across the grain.

Smoked Maple Prime Rib

Ingredients

1 (6 pound) three-rib standing rib roast, bones separated from the roast and tied in place

coarse sea salt to taste

coarsely ground black pepper to taste

3 cups maple wood chips

Directions

Soak wood chips in water until fully moistened, at least 1 hour.

Preheat smoker to 225 degrees F (110 degrees C). Place a drip pan beneath the rack where you will roast the meat.

Season roast generously with sea salt and black pepper to coat on all sides; rub seasoning into the meat and fat.

Put the roast into the preheated smoker above the drip pan with the fat cap facing upwards.

Add 2/3 cup of the soaked wood chips to your heat source according to your smoker's instruction manual.

Smoke the roast in the preheated smoker for 30 minutes. Add half the remaining wood chips to the heat source. Smoke another 30 minutes and add remainder of the wood chips. Continue smoking roast until browned on the outside and red in the center, about 2 hours more. An instant-read thermometer inserted into the center should read 125 degrees F (49 degrees C).

Remove roast to a cutting board, cover loosely with aluminum foil, and rest beef for 30 minutes. Carve into 1/2- to 1-inch slices.

Smoked Mesquite Beef Brisket

Ingredients

5 pounds beef brisket, trimmed of fat

3 tablespoons mustard, or as needed

2 tablespoons brisket rub, or as needed

Mesquite wood

Directions

Coat beef brisket with mustard. Cover with brisket rub. Let marinate in the refrigerate, 8 hours to overnight.

Remove brisket from the refrigerator and bring to room temperature.

Preheat a smoker to 220 degrees F (104 degrees F) according to manufacturer's instructions.

Place beef brisket in the smoker and smoke until easily pierced with a knife and an instant-read thermometer inserted into the center reads 190 degrees F (88 degrees C), 6 1/4 to 7 1/2 hours.

Wrap brisket with aluminum foil and let rest for 30 minutes before slicing.

Cayenne BBQ Beef Ribs

Ingredients

1 rack beef ribs, centre cut or back

2 tbsp paprika

2 tbsp sugar

1 tbsp salt

1 tbsp chili powder

1 tbsp garlic powder

1 1/2 tsp dry mustard

1 tsp black pepper

1 tsp oregano

1 tsp cumin

1/2 tsp cayenne pepper

1 cup bbq sauce

Directions

Mix the spices and sugar together to make the seasoning mixture.

Peel the membrane off the back of the ribs. Generously rub the seasoning mixture all over the ribs. Place in the fridge for 2-3 hours.

Set smoker to 250F using mesquite or other wood chips. Place the ribs in the smoker and smoke for 3 hours.

Remove the ribs from the smoker and generously coat the ribs with bbq sauce. Let them rest for 10 minutes before cutting and serving.

Smoked Black Pepper Beef Brisket

Ingredients

1 beef brisket

2 tbsp salt

3 tbsp freshly cracked black pepper

1 tbsp chili powder

1 tbsp garlic powder

2 tsp onion powder

2 tsp cayenne pepper

2 tsp white sugar

Directions

Rub the salt all over the brisket. Cover with plastic wrap and place in the fridge for 30 minutes.

Make the rub by mixing together the sugar and all the remaining spices. Generously rub the spice mixture all over the brisket.

Set the smoker to 225F using mesquite wood.

Smoke the brisket, with the fat cap facing up, until it reaches an internal temperature of 195F. Slice and serve.

Juicy Smoked Sirloin

Ingredients

1 top sirloin beef roast (5-6 pounds)

3 tbsp sea salt

1/4 cup Montreal steak spice

Directions

Trim the roast of any excess fat. If desired, tie the roast up with kitchen twine.

Rub the roast down with the sea salt and then rub the roast with the Montreal steak spice. Set up smoker for 250F using mesquite wood, or other wood of choice.

Lay the roast on a smoker rack and smoke until 135F, or until desired doneness. Remove the roast from the smoker and let rest for 10 minutes.

Slice and serve.

Smoked Cola BBQ Beef Ribs

Ingredients

2 (3 1/2-lb.) racks beef back ribs

1/3 cup kosher salt

1/4 cup finely ground medium-roast coffee beans

3 tablespoons black pepper

2 tablespoons paprika

2 tablespoons chili powder

2 handfulls wood chips for smoking

Cola BBQ Sauce

1 cup cola soft drink

1 cup ketchup

1/2 cup brewed coffee

1/4 cup dark molasses

2 tablespoons sherry vinegar

2 tablespoons Worcestershire sauce

1/2 teaspoon chili powder

1/2 teaspoon kosher salt

1/8 teaspoon garlic powder

1/8 teaspoon onion powder

Directions

Pat both sides of slabs dry with paper towels. Using a sharp knife, remove thin membrane from back of each by slicing into it and pulling it off with a paper towel.

Combine salt, coffee, pepper, paprika, and chili powder in a bowl; rub evenly over both sides of each rack, and let stand at room temperature 30 minutes.

Make the Cola BBQ Sauce:

Combine all the ingredients for in a medium saucepan over medium-low. Cook, stirring occasionally, until heated through and flavors meld, about 30 minutes. Remove from heat, and cool completely, about 30 minutes.

Prepare a charcoal fire in smoker according to manufacturer's instructions, bringing internal temperature to 250°F to 275°F. Maintain temperature for 15 to 20 minutes. Place wood chunks on coals.

Place ribs, meaty side up, on smoker; cover with lid. Smoke ribs, maintaining inside temperature between 250°F and 275°F, until meat begins to pull away from bones but is not yet tender, about 3 hours. Brush about 1/2 cup Cola-Coffee BBQ Sauce over both sides of ribs.

Cover and smoke until a meat thermometer inserted in between the rib bones registers 205°F and rib meat is very tender, about 1 hour and 30 minutes, brushing with about 1/4 cup barbecue sauce every 30 minutes.

Remove ribs from the smoker; brush with 1/4 cup barbecue sauce. Serve with remaining barbecue sauce.

Chapter 3: Smoked Chicken And Turkey Recipes

Spicy Smoked Chicken Wings

Ingredients

3 pounds chicken wings

2 tablespoons Cajun seasoning, or as needed

2 tablespoons butter

2 tablespoons minced garlic

2 tablespoons Cajun seasoning

16 ounces hot sauce

4 cups vegetable oil, or as needed

3 cups hickory wood chips, divided

Directions

Preheat smoker to 200 degrees F (95 degrees C) and add 1 cup wood chips to start the smoke rolling.

Liberally coat chicken wings with about 2 tablespoons Cajun seasoning.

Place wings directly on the grate in the smoker or in an aluminum pan with holes to allow airflow. Add more wood chips as needed to continue smoke. Smoke wings for 2 hours.

Combine butter, garlic, and 2 tablespoons Cajun seasoning in a large saucepan over medium-low heat; cook and stir until butter is melted, about 1 minute. Stir hot sauce into butter mixture; simmer, stirring occasionally, until sauce has thickened, about 30 minutes.

Heat oil in a deep-fryer or large saucepan to 375 degrees F (190 degrees C).

Preheat grill to 375 degrees F (190 degrees C).

Cook wings, 10 to 12 at a time, in the deep fryer until no wings are longer pink in the center and are lightly browned on the outside, 5 to 7 minutes. Remove wings from the oil with a slotted spoon, letting excess oil drain from the wings.

Place cooked wings on a baking sheet and liberally coat each wing with hot sauce mixture.

Place coated wings directly onto the grates of the preheated grill; cook until sauce has caramelized and wings are crisp, 2 to 3 minutes per side.

Smoked Cola Turkey

Ingredients

1 (10 pound) whole turkey, neck and giblets removed

4 cloves garlic, crushed

2 tablespoons seasoned salt

1/2 cup butter

2 (12 fluid ounce) cans cola-flavored carbonated beverage

1 apple, quartered

1 onion, quartered

1 tablespoon garlic powder

1 tablespoon salt

1 tablespoon ground black pepper

Directions

Preheat smoker to 225 to 250 degrees F (110 to 120 degrees C).

Rinse turkey under cold water, and pat dry. Rub the crushed garlic over the outside of the bird, and sprinkle with seasoned salt. Place in a disposable roasting pan.

Fill turkey cavity with butter, cola, apple, onion, garlic powder, salt, and ground black pepper. Cover loosely with foil.

Smoke at 225 to 250 degrees F (110 to 120 degrees C) for 10 hours, or until internal temperature reaches 180 degrees F (80 degrees C) when measured in the thickest part of the thigh.

Baste the bird every 1 to 2 hours with the juices from the bottom of the roasting pan.

Smoked Chicken With Herbs

Ingredients

1 (4 pound) whole chicken

3 tablespoons butter

1 tablespoon chopped fresh parsley

1 tablespoon chopped fresh oregano

1 tablespoon chopped fresh basil

1 tablespoon fresh chives, finely chopped

Directions

Preheat an outdoor grill for low heat.

Rinse chicken inside and out. Pat dry. Loosen skin around the breast area.

Place three tablespoons of butter in various places under the skin. Mix herbs together and place half under the skin and the other half inside the chicken.

Cook chicken with smoke for 4 hours or until juices run clear when poked with a fork.

Smoked Honey Turkey

Ingredients

1 (12 pound) whole turkey

2 tablespoons chopped fresh sage

2 tablespoons ground black pepper

2 tablespoons celery salt

2 tablespoons chopped fresh basil

2 tablespoons vegetable oil

1 (12 ounce) jar honey

1/2 pound mesquite wood chips

Directions

Preheat grill for high heat. If you are using a charcoal grill, use about twice the normal amount of charcoal. Soak wood chips in a pan of water, and set next to the grill.

Remove neck and giblets from turkey. Rinse the bird and pat dry. Place in a large disposable roasting pan.

In a medium bowl, mix together sage, ground black pepper, celery salt, basil, and vegetable oil. Pour mixture evenly over the turkey. Turn the turkey breast side down in the pan, and tent loosely with aluminum foil.

Place the roasting pan on the preheated grill. Throw a handful of the wood chips onto the coals. Close the lid, and cook for 1 hour.

Throw about 2 more handfuls of soaked wood chips on the fire. Drizzle 1/2 the honey over the bird, and replace the foil. Close the lid of the grill, and continue cooking 1 1/2 to 2 hours, or until internal temperature reaches 180 degrees F (80 degrees C) in the thickest part of the thigh.

Uncover turkey, and carefully turn it breast side up in the roasting pan. Baste with remaining honey. Leave the turkey uncovered, and cook 15 minutes. The cooked honey will be very dark.

Smoked Mesquite Chicken Wings

Ingredients

16 chicken wings, tips discarded

1/4 cup olive oil

1/4 cup dry rub for chicken

1 pound mesquite wood chips, soaked in water

1 (8 ounce) bottle blue cheese salad dressing

Directions

Place chicken wings in a large bowl. Pour in olive oil; toss with hands until coated. Coat wings evenly with dry rub.

Light charcoal and heat smoker to 170 to 200 degrees F (77 to 93 degrees C) according to manufacturer's instructions.

Drain wood chips and place half of them directly on the charcoal. Spread wings evenly on the cooking grate skin-side down.

Smoke wings until fragrant, about 1 hour.

Flip wings. Add remaining wood chips to the charcoal. Continue smoking until an instant-read thermometer inserted near the bone reads 165 degrees F (74 degrees C), about 1 hour more.

Serve chicken wings with blue cheese dressing.

Smoked Black Peppercorn Chicken Wings

Ingredients

3 tablespoons whole black peppercorns

2 tablespoons coriander seeds

2 tablespoons mustard seeds

1 tablespoon fennel seeds

1 tablespoon cumin seeds

4 cups water

1 onion, diced

8 cloves garlic, smashed

1 (2 inch) piece fresh ginger, sliced

2 tablespoons dried rosemary

2 tablespoons dried thyme

6 bay leaves

1/2 cup white sugar

1/3 cup salt

3 pounds chicken wings, tips removed and sections separated

2 lemons, zested and juiced

2 limes, zested and juiced

ice cubes (optional)

1 (64 fluid ounce) bottle apple juice

applewood chips, soaked

vegetable oil for frying

Directions

Combine peppercorns, coriander, mustard, fennel, and cumin in a mortar and pestle; crush until fragrant and just broken.

Bring water to a boil in a saucepan. Add peppercorn-seed mixture, onion, garlic, ginger, rosemary, thyme, and bay leaves; bring back to a boil. Reduce heat to low; simmer until flavors meld, about 25 minutes. Cool brine, about 10 minutes.

Pour 2 cups brine into a large 10-quart plastic container with a tight-fitting lid. Stir in sugar and salt until dissolved. Add chicken wings, lemon zest and juice, and lime zest and juice.

Drop ice into the pot with the remaining brine to cool it down. Pour into the plastic container. Add enough apple juice to cover the wings. Stir well and seal container; refrigerate for 24 to 48 hours.

Preheat smoker to 275 to 300 degrees F (135 to 150 degrees C) according to manufacturer's directions.

Rinse wings under cold tap water; dry, unstacked, on wire racks. Place the racks into the smoker. Add applewood chips according to manufacturer's directions. Smoke until chicken develops a smoky flavor but is not fully cooked, about 25 minutes. Transfer wings to a tray and pat dry with paper towels.

Heat oil in a deep-fryer or large saucepan to 350 degrees F (175 degrees C). Fry wings, 8 to 10 at a time, until golden brown and crispy, 60 to 90 seconds.

Smoked Paprika Chicken

Ingredients

1 large whole chicken (4 pounds)

2 teaspoon salt

2 teaspoons black pepper

2 teaspoons paprika

2 teaspoons dried thyme

2 teaspoons garlic salt

2 teaspoons lemon pepper

2 teaspoons cayenne pepper

6 tablespoons olive oil

Hickory wood chips

Apple wood chips

Directions

Soak your hickory and apple wood chips in water for a couple hours to allow them to smoulder instead of burn out quickly. Use half hickory and apple wood for smoking.

Mix all of the chicken seasonings together in a mixing bowl and rub on the chicken.

Light your smoker until it warms to 250F. Place the chicken breasts on your smoker and shut your grill lid. Leave the vents on your smoker at least a quarter of a turn open.

Check your chicken after an hour to make sure it is cooking correctly and that the temperature in your smoker is still holding at about 250 F. Add additional hickory and apple wood if needed.

Total cooking time for a whole chicken will be 3-4 hours (depending on chicken size). Check the internal temperature of the chicken with a meat thermometer making sure chicken is 160F in center of chicken.

Once you remove chicken off the smoker, make sure to wrap a foil tent around it for at least 20 minutes to let it rest.

Smoked Italian Chicken Legs

Ingredients

1 (3 1/2 lb) chicken legs or thighs

½ cup Italian salad dressing

½ cup soy sauce

¼ cup barbecue spice

2 cups apple juice

Directions

Rinse chicken with cold water and pat dry.

Mix salad dressing and soy sauce in a bowl; strain. Inject chicken with salad dressing mixture.

Sprinkle barbeque seasoning evenly over chicken.

Place chicken in sealable plastic bag; seal bag.

Marinate in the refrigerator for 8 hours or longer. Remove chicken from bag.

Cook chicken in smoker at 250 degrees F over indirect heat for 4 hours or until cooked through, misting with apple juice every 30 minutes.

Use hickory chips or apple wood in the smoker.

Smoked BBQ Chicken Legs

Ingredients

2 (12 fluid ounce) cans beer

2 cups hickory wood chips, or as much as you like

4 chicken leg quarters

2 cups barbeque sauce

salt and pepper to taste

heavy duty aluminum foil

Directions

Preheat an outdoor grill for medium heat. Coat the grill surface lightly with oil. Pour beer into a pan or bowl, and add wood chips. Let soak while the grill heats up.

When the coals are ready, sprinkle the hickory chips over them. Place chicken pieces on the grill, cover, and cook for 15 minutes. Turnover, cover and grill for an additional 15 minutes.

Remove the chicken pieces from the grill, and place each leg quarter onto a large square of aluminum foil. Cover with barbeque sauce, and fold the foil into a packet around each piece of chicken.

Return chicken packets to the grill, and cook for an additional 15 minutes per side. Remove packets, and serve with more barbeque sauce.

Printed in Great Britain
by Amazon